Open the Door to My Presence

Open the Door to My Presence

Jacqueline Varnedoe

ISBN# 978-0-9843121-4-6

Published and distributed by:	*Calling to Excellence, Inc.* *Thomasville, GA 31792* *Email: varnedoe@rose.net*
Editor/Publishing & Design Director:	*Margie Knight,* *KnightWriter-2-Publish* *Email: knightwriter2publish@gmail.com*
Interior Design Credit:	*Janet Long* *Janet Long Design* *Email: jalolong1@yahoo.com*
Cover Design Credit:	*Mindy Faubion,* *Faubion Creative Studios* *Email: mindyfaubion@yahoo.com*
Printed in:	*USA*

Worldwide distribution

Endorsements

In today's generation, God is rebuilding the Tabernacle of David. That Tabernacle, which is filled with praise, wells deep within each of us. The presence of a holy God is meant to burn like a lamp to a world that is weary. Jacqueline Varnedoe captures how to open the door to God's presence in you. In a season when the Spirit of God is knocking at the door of the hearts of His people, *Open the Door to My Presence* is a must read. Not only does Jacqueline recount key experiences to help us understand how to open the door to the presence of God, but she also gives us key principles to the mystery of God in us. When you read this book, you will feel like you have come to the table of the Lord.

Dr. Chuck D. Pierce
President, Global Spheres Inc.
President, Glory of Zion Intl.

Powerful words leap off the pages and into your heart as you read *Open the Door to My Presence*! Jacqueline Varnedoe has an amazing way of capturing the heart of God in her book. She helps the reader to experience a personal conversation with God. As you read the book, God pours out His plan for your life. You, then, are able to respond to the awesome Presence of the Lord. I recommend *Open the Door to My Presence* for anyone hungry for a personal encounter with the Lord. Your life will forever be changed!

Barbara Wentroble
President – International Breakthrough Ministries
President – Business Owners for Christ International

We are living in tumultuous times. Warfare is increasing. In these days, God wants to raise His people up to experience a new level of His power and glory. In *Open the Door to My Presence*, Jacqueline Varnedoe challenges her readers to go beyond the ordinary; to experience the full expression of the Spirit's manifold ministry and literally become a carrier of His Presence! May this book bless you and bring you to a new experience of God's glory! May you never be the same!

Dr. Robert Heidler
Apostolic Teacher
Glory of Zion International Ministries

"In her book, *Open the Door to My Presence*, Jacqueline Varnedoe creates a step-by-step pathway into a deeper relationship with God. She takes you past the surface level of salvation, into the deeper waters of the Holy Spirit and finally into the depths of the glory of His presence. This is the goal in the heart of God for every believer."

Linda Heidler
Apostolic Prayer Minister
Glory of Zion International Ministries

Since *Open the Door to My Presence* was written in the first person, I felt like God was speaking directly to me; and I found myself talking back to Him throughout the book. When God knows we are ready to receive, He illuminates the words, which He did for me as I read each chapter. If He did it for me, He will do it for others.

Dianne Keller
Prayer Warrior

In *Open the Door to My Presence* Jacqueline Varnedoe draws readers into a realm that captures the true heart of God the Father rarely experienced in today's world. Each of Jacqueline's previous books, Come Walk With Me and Joy Carriers, moved believers to a greater level of intimacy and truth many had never encountered. Open the Door to My Presence now offers challenges that climax at a level of intimacy in Him that is desperately needed in the critical times we are facing. I can promise that you will be forever changed by the time you finish reading this book.

Margie Knight
Writer/Editor
KnightWriter-2-Publish

Dedication

*I*t is my joy to dedicate this book to my children and grandchildren. You are the ones that will be His torch carriers long after I have finished my race.

My prayer for each of you is that your greatest desire will be to seek first the kingdom of God and to love Him more each day.

So as Papa said to each of us, I say now to my children—Jacqueline and Robert Morgan, Rand and Elizabeth Malone, Heeth IV and Susan Varnedoe, and Howard and Dawn Varnedoe: "KEEP THE FIRE BURNING."

Then pass the torch to my grandchildren—Morgan and Krishan Purvis; David and Randolph Malone; Ann and Heeth Varnedoe V; and Joshua, Andrew, Ashley, Phillip and Katie Varnedoe. May you continue to grow each day in the grace and knowledge of the Lord Jesus Christ.

Acknowledgements

First of all, I humbly thank Abba Father for His love, His direction and His words as I penned this book.

A special thanks is extended to Chuck Pierce for confirming that this book was a part of Father's plan and not just a good idea.

Margie Knight was a gem with her editing skills and many thanks and much appreciation go to her.

Susan Huddleston: thank you for taking the time to read and edit several chapters.

To my family: thank you for your many prayers through the months of writing and going to press. You are truly special jewels to me. I love each of you, and I am so grateful for our family prayer list.

My thanks and deep appreciation extends to my brother and sister-in-love, Bill and Joann Ponder. You have been such a support with book signings of my other two books, help with delivery and your many prayers.

To my special friends that always asked about the book, prayed and truly carried me through this process; thank you so much.

To our House of Zion: thank you for your love and encouragement throughout this project.

Special thanks go to my husband, Heeth Varnedoe III, for his patience on the days that I was on overload.

Table of Contents

Introduction

alking with the Lord is truly an exciting adventure. He is full of surprises and little nudges that you cannot ignore. Well, you could ignore them, but not if your heart is to please Him.

If you have read either one of my books, *COME WALK WITH ME* or *JOY CARRIERS*, you will know that my heart's desire is to know Him and to love Him. Continuing to grow in intimacy is the joy and challenge of my life.

I heard a well-known minister say, "You can either be a voice or an echo." In other words, if you have not truly walked in what you are teaching or writing, you will just be an echo of what someone else has experienced.

I believe that the Lord never calls us to do something, without first preparing everything that we need to complete the task. So as I seek His face, I am excited about what He is going to reveal to all of us.

I invite you to join me as we pursue opening the door to an even greater awareness of His Presence. Together we will discover the keys needed to unlock not just one door but many doors as we grow and mature in our walk with the Lord.

As I always tell my readers, you are all in different places in your relationship with Him. If you have questions or uncertainties, then ask the Lord for clarity but keep walking. If some parts seem elementary just refuel what you already know and continue to read. ALL OF YOU WILL BE GLAD THAT YOU FINISHED THE JOURNEY.

In this hour, Abba Father is calling a people who desire Him above all else—a people who truly are seeking first the Kingdom of God.

Our Prayer and Response

Father, thank You for the invitation to come into Your presence. What an inspiring invitation from such an awesome God we serve. The fact that anyone would hesitate to accept Your invitation, only shows the lack of true understanding of Your heart. There is no greater love than Your love for us. So, with abundant joy and expectancy we answer Your call as we open up our hearts and let You in.

Prologue

have chosen to use the literary style of first person in this book, thereby allowing the heart of Father God to speak directly to you. I prayed earnestly to hear His voice in order to become a vessel to share the thoughts and intents of His heart with you.

As you read, let His words penetrate your very being. It is important that you listen with your heart and not just read the words. Please take time to allow Him to teach you and show you His ways.

He is a many-faceted God. His joy is to reveal Himself to each individual as He chooses. One person may see and reap a truth that another cannot yet comprehend.

We begin our spiritual journey taking baby steps and gradually evolve into maturity. To grow into a deeper level of relationship, we must yield to our Lord. He prepares us by working in the daily circumstances of our life experiences. Our part is to submit ourselves unconditionally to Him and then cooperate with Him in whatever He may do in us.

One of the purposes of this book is to cause us to turn aside. The concept of "turning aside" is very close to the heart of the Lord, who greatly desires that we both notice and respond to His Presence.

The Lord revealed Himself to Moses in a flame of fire. Thus, the bush burned but was not consumed. It can be said that the bush is yet burning and available to us.

And Moses said, "I will now turn aside, and see this great sight, why the bush is not burnt." [1]

Simply pray and follow Moses' example by turning aside to see and embrace God's manifested presence.

Our Prayer and Response

Precious Lord, we willingly turn aside and embrace the words you are speaking to us. We ask for ears to hear Your voice and hearts to receive Your words. Thank You for desiring our presence. We are eternally grateful for the blood of Jesus, which makes it all possible. We love You and ask You to help us delve into the wisdom You are about to share with us.

Chapter 1

God Had A Plan

In the beginning God created the heavens and the earth.

Genesis 1:1

efore creation, I had a plan. You were part of that plan—even then you were in My heart. I anticipated the day that I would form your inward parts and cover you in your mother's womb.

Your frame was not hidden from Me when you were made in secret. In My Book, the days fashioned for you were already written. Before you were conceived, I knew you.

Part of My plan was to have a people that would desire My Presence. Truly, the cry of My heart is intimacy in relationship. In the garden, this was the bond that I enjoyed with Adam and Eve.

I was delighted to witness the excitement in Adam's eyes when I first introduced him to the animal kingdom. He was like a little child going from animal to animal trying to decide what to call each one. As Adam gave names to the cattle, to the birds of the air, and to every beast of the field; My heart rejoiced to see the joy on his face.

Then I knew that the time had come for me to make Adam a helper comparable to him. So I caused a deep sleep to fall on Adam, and I took one of his ribs and made a woman.

Adam said, "This is now bone of my bones and flesh of my flesh, she shall be called Woman because she was taken out of Man."[1]

The three of us took many walks together in the garden. As we walked, I shared My heart with them and taught them My ways. During these times, I commanded them, saying, "Of every tree of the garden you may freely eat; but of the tree of the knowledge of good and evil you shall not eat, for in the day that you eat of it you shall truly die."[2]

Ponder the fact that they could eat of every tree but one! However, the enemy tempted Eve and she disobeyed and ate the apple. Then as the Scriptures tell you, she gave to Adam and he ate.

You might think, *Why, when they had all the other trees from which to choose, did they have to eat that apple?* They were deceived by the serpent into thinking; "Hath God really said?" Then once that door of doubt was opened, they stepped into the trap satan had planned for them. At the time, taking and eating the fruit seemed more appealing than worrying about the consequences. However, for Adam and Eve, life would never be the same. Their moment of disobedience affected all mankind.

How many times, My children, have you read this account of Adam and Eve in the garden? Have you ever truly grasped how painful this was for Me? Yes, I am the great I AM but never forget that I desire intimacy with My children. I am Abba Father and I love deeply.

I watched as they ran and hid among the trees. My heart broke, knowing that our relationship would be changed forever. So many times before, they had run to embrace Me. Together we would have a depth of conversation that is possible only with those people that have a bond of love and trust.

I called, 'Where are you?' Of course, I knew where they were hiding, but it was necessary that they answer my call. I had to confront them with the truth—the penalty for their disobedience.

Adam replied, "I heard Your voice in the garden, and I was afraid because I was naked, and I hid myself."[3]

I responded, "Who told you that you were naked? Have you eaten from the tree of which I commanded you that you should not eat?"[4]

There are many things that you may not understand. However, you must never forget this fact. When I ask you not to do something, it is for your own welfare. I know the end from the beginning and the beginning from the end. What I require from you in obedience comes from a heart of love.

The result of all sin is despair, discouragement and disappointment. The apple may have tasted good for a moment, but the end result was spiritual death.

The fig leaves with which they had clothed themselves had to be discarded. I took tunics of skin and clothed them. Then I watched as they walked out of the garden.

Adam and Eve were arguing as they walked, blaming each other for what had happened. Shame was written on their faces. Gone was the peace that they had previously enjoyed together and with Me.

My Father-heart was crushed, knowing all that was ahead for them. The bond of friendship that we had enjoyed was broken. It would never be the same between us.

However, one thing I knew, nothing could stop the fulfillment of My plan. That fact gave Me joy in the pain of the moment.

❖ ❖ ❖

Prayerfully meditate on this song and then ask yourself: Can I stay where I am? Am I willing to go on the journey that never ends?

THE JOURNEY

Deep calls unto deep

At the sound of Your rivers raging in me

I can only move with the rhythms

Of the grace that has captured me

I sleep but my heart is awakened

How can I stay where I am?

How can I stay where I've been?

CHORUS

I'm running after You

I'm running hard, and the day is breaking

Letting go of what I've known or what is true,

Here I am, fill me once again

And take me on this journey with you.

Lord, take me on this journey with you

That never ends.

VERSE TWO

Deep calls unto deep

At the sounds of your heart, beating in me

I am not afraid of the sound

Of the voice that's calling me

I sleep but my heart is awakened

How can I stay where I've been?[5]

❖ ❖ ❖

OUR PRAYER AND RESPONSE

Father God—Abba—we come to You with hearts filled with gratefulness. Even before You created the Earth, You had a plan. You knew that man would not resist the temptation in the garden. Jesus was Your plan. By His blood, we are cleansed and set free from the bondages of sin. We can now enter freely into

Your presence. It is with great joy that we answer Your call and let You enter our hearts.

Chapter 2

I Am Knocking At The Door

*Behold, I stand at the door and knock, if any-
one hears My voice and opens the door, I will
come in to him and dine with him, and he
with Me.*

Revelation 3:20

I am standing at the door and I am knocking. Can you
hear Me calling your name? If you hear, open the door. I
am waiting. My heart's desire is to come and spend time
with you to escort you through one door then another door and
then another door.

Many people over the years have been confused when they
read this verse. Having accepted Jesus, as their Lord and Savior,
they did not understand that I was urging them to go beyond the
salvation experience.

When you responded to my first knock; I touched your heart
and covered you with the blood of My Son, Jesus—the Christ.

You entered My Kingdom and became My child.

However, the journey does not stop with the opening of the first door. Come, hear My voice calling you. Now is the time to stretch out and reach beyond where you have been.

The path is becoming narrower, and you need the light of My Spirit to illumine the way. I am the LIGHT of the world—he that walks with Me shall not walk in darkness but shall have the light of life.

Often My children come to Me only with requests and desires. This becomes a one-way conversation that lacks any depth. They fail to stop and listen and, therefore, don't learn how to hear and distinguish My voice.

This is a time to look beyond. Seek Me with all your heart and you will find Me. I will show you My heart. I yearn for intimacy with you.

The enemy of your soul is saying, "Stop right here. Why do you want to leave what is comfortable to go after the unknown?" Just as he tempted Eve, the enemy is tempting you saying, "You know how blessed you are. Just think, you can have your cake and eat it, too. Did you not already accept Jesus? Why would you want more? You could lose your job or your friends if you get too involved with all that religion. You certainly don't want to ruin your good reputation!"

Precious Ones, let Me remind you what My Son told His disciples: "It was necessary for Me to suffer, and to rise from the dead the third day, and that repentance and remission of sins should be preached in My name to all nations, beginning at

Jerusalem. And you are witnesses to these things. Behold, I send the Promise of My Father upon you: but tarry in the city of Jerusalem until you are endued with power from on high."[1]

The disciples had walked with Jesus for three years. However, even the disciples, except perhaps John, didn't experience intimacy with Him. He gave them power and authority over all demons and to cure diseases. He sent them to preach the kingdom of God and to heal the sick.

However, they needed more! They needed to be endued with the power of Holy Spirit. Yes, they had acknowledged that He was the Messiah, but that alone was not enough. They needed the resurrection power My Son paid for at the cross.

Remember, I am the God that created the universe. My plan extends across the ages; and in that plan, you are a part. Everything that you will ever need to finish the race, I have already prepared.

This is the point of great decision. Through the years, religion has blinded My people from seeing the next door. Their hearts have been closed to believing that I desire to instruct and teach them in the way that they should go. They have not comprehended or truly understood that I am a God that is calling their name and saying, "Let Me capture your heart."

Today I am inviting you to open the next door. As you open the door and enter in, you will find the place that I have prepared for you. Don't you understand that I alone know your heart? As you sit with Me, I will encourage, teach and enlighten you.

To open or not open the door is not My choice but yours. You can keep the door closed; and as long as you allow Me to live in your heart, you will enter heaven when you leave this earth. However, you will not have finished the race that I set before you.

I have so much to show you and impart into you. However, know that this is not for you alone. There are people that I have predestined for you to reach. They are waiting to hear all that I will give you to speak to them. If only My family would truly understand that every joint supplies. What I have given you to do, will not be completed, or it will be delayed if you do not answer the call.

Father's heart is crying out to you. Ask yourself these questions: Am I willing to give Him my all? Can I risk remaining where I am or will I allow Him to capture my heart?

Now pause briefly to meditate on the following Scripture:

"Enter by the narrow gate; for wide is the gate and broad is the way that leads to destruction, and there are many who go in by it. Because narrow is the gate and difficult is the way which leads to life, and there are few who find it."

Matthew 7:13-14

OUR PRAYER AND RESPONSE

Father God, as I began the journey on this straight and narrow path, I wanted to stop. The wide path looked much more inviting— like a big party and everyone seemed to be having so much fun. However, I remember you told me in the beginning that there were many doors to open. Somehow I knew that the next door to be opened was on this path—the straight and narrow. I pray now, Abba Father, for the grace to keep walking on Your chosen path. This is Your way for me.

Chapter 3

The Door To My Power

*But you shall receive power when the Holy
Spirit has come upon you; and you shall be
witnesses to Me in Jerusalem, and in all Judea
and Samaria, and to the end of the earth.*

Acts 1:8

gain, I am reminding you what Jesus spoke to His disciples: "Do not depart from Jerusalem, but wait for the Promise of the Father, for John truly baptized with water, but you shall be baptized with the Holy Spirit not many days from now."[1]

There was so much that I desired to do through the disciples, but it could not be done without My power. Just as today—I am calling My people to an even higher realm of authority—My power is available if they will, by faith, let it flow in and through them.

As you spend time in My Presence, as we fellowship together, My heart begins to flow into you. Then there begins to grow a seed of understanding of the greatness of the authority that I have placed upon you.

At a moment in time after Jesus was resurrected, He appeared to the eleven disciples as they sat at the table. He rebuked their unbelief and hardness of heart, because they did not believe those who had seen Him after He had risen.

Jesus spoke to them saying, "Go into all the world and preach the gospel to every creature. He who believes and is baptized will be saved; but he who does not believe will be condemned. And these signs will follow those who believe: In My name they will cast out demons; they will speak with new tongues." [2]

He even told them they would take up serpents; and if they drank anything deadly, it would by no means hurt them.

He commissioned them just as I am calling you today to lay hands on the sick and believe that they will recover. My children, if My Son rebuked His disciples for their unbelief and hardness of heart; will I not also rebuke you? Many of you have been taught the truth of My Word for years and yet you, too, still walk in doubt and unbelief.

Also, if you truly knew My heart, you would not take My Word out of context. You would remember that when the serpent attached itself to Paul, he shook it off into the fire. He was not harmed by the bite, because He knew that I was the Healer. However, he did not test Me by playing with serpents.

You are thinking, but Lord, we would never play with serpents. No, and neither has your faith risen to believe that you could respond as Paul did. It might not be a serpent bite, but it could be a challenging assignment. The question I pose to you is this: whose report will you believe?

If you accidentally drink or eat something poisonous, can I not tell you, as I told Elisha, what to do?

Elisha had learned to hear My voice. It was while the sons of the prophets were eating the stew that they cried out, "Man of God, there is death in the pot." So Elisha said, "Then bring some flour." And he put it into the pot, and said, "Serve it to the people, that they may eat." And there was nothing harmful in the pot.

You learn My ways as you and I spend time together apart from the busyness of the world. Many have walked in My power, but they have walked away from intimacy with Me. That is why in this hour, I am calling a people—the Triumphant Reserve—to prepare them for such a time as this. They will be a people that truly desire to dwell in the secret place with Me. Their first priority is to seek first My Kingdom.

The door that you have opened to My power can poison your heart if it is just the power and prestige that you seek and not My heart.

Does not My Word say—it is not by might nor by power, but by My Spirit?[3] Often My people get confused. They begin to flow in the gifts of the Spirit and see miracles—blind eyes are opened, the lame walk, the sick are healed—but they forget it is not by their power or gifting but by My Spirit working through them.

Can you not see or understand that intimacy with Me is not just a desire of My heart? It is essential for your total well-being.

Come with Me into the living room of one who meets with Me every morning. After years of time spent together, he has learned that intimacy is not just about the words spoken in prayer. I am waiting with excitement for the fellowship that we will enjoy. My Father-heart is yearning for this special exchange of silent communication. I know that I am loved!

His name is John and he chose years ago to continue to open the door—yes, door after door. Now he is content just to be with Me. Many days he leaves with assignments that I have for him. Then there are days that he departs from our times together, satisfied that he has blessed Me with precious fellowship from one of My children.

Perfection is not what I am seeking in My family. If you love Me, you will keep My commandments. It will not be bondage to walk with Me but great joy.

Power—yes, you must believe that I have given you all power. If I call you to do something, then I will equip you for the task. Often the key is whether you believe that I have called you for such a time as this. You must grasp hold of My truth—all power has been given to you to complete what I have called you to do.

You will never arrive. It is a lifelong process. However, remember that I have begun a good work in you, which will continue until the day of Jesus Christ's return.

Pause now and thank Abba Father for the power and presence of the Holy Spirit. Then ask yourself these questions: Will I allow Him to change my heart by the grace He instills in me? Am I ready and willing to draw close to Him and wait for an even greater impartation of His love and power?

❖ ❖ ❖

OUR PRAYER AND RESPONSE

Father God, we stand in awe of You. Thank You, Abba, for giving strength and power to Your people. You are mighty and yet full of loving-kindness.

When first we meet You as our Lord and Savior, our hearts cannot understand the greatness of Your love and power. How good You are to take us one step at a time. You are patient and don't force us or pressure us to open the next door. You wait in the shadows, praying that we will soon hear and obey. Your Spirit leads us on in the power of Your love.

Chapter 4

The Manifold Spirit Of God

The Spirit of the Lord shall rest upon Him; the Spirit of wisdom and understanding, the Spirit of counsel and might, the Spirit of knowledge and of the fear of the Lord.

Isaiah 11:2

he seven Spirits of God depict Holy Spirit in His perfect dynamic display of power. Unfortunately, you often limit Me by trying to understand with the natural mind what can only be comprehended by the Spirit. Listen to Me, and I will teach you step-by-step and precept-upon-precept.

You were filled with the Spirit of the Lord as you waited in My Presence—just as the 120 were filled as they tarried in the City of Jerusalem. However, there is so much more that I desire to reveal to you. A deeper comprehension of the fullness of Holy Spirit will be uncovered as you linger with Me.

Through the ages many of My people have desired My Presence above all else. Moses refused to go on unless My Presence went with him. As he was with Me on the mountain, I passed before him and proclaimed, "I AM the Lord, the Lord God, merciful and gracious, long suffering and abounding in goodness and truth."

Enoch was My friend. His greatest joy was to walk and talk with Me. The day came when the path on which He walked came closer and closer, and I simply allowed him to walk behind the veil and enter into to his heavenly home.

David was a worshipper and a man after My own heart. When he sinned with Bathsheba and was confronted by the prophet, his reply was not, "Please do not take my kingdom." No, he cried out, "Create in me a clean heart, O God, and renew a steadfast spirit within me. Do not cast me away from Your presence, and do not take Your Holy Spirit from me."[1]

The disciples of Jesus loved Me. However, it was only after His death and resurrection that they truly understood how much I loved them. When they were filled with My Spirit and My power at Pentecost, their eyes were opened to see with My eyes. The fire of Holy Spirit was covering them and resting upon them.

I sincerely desire for you to be a people of My Presence. As you go out into the world, a supernatural glow will be upon you that will draw others to Me. As My Spirit flows through you, then the fruit of My Spirit will be seen in you—My love, joy peace, longsuffering, kindness, goodness, and faithfulness. However, just as with the growth of natural fruit, the seed is planted; but it takes years before the fruit appears on the branches. My people that are willing to spend quality time with Me day-after-day are those that will display My fruit.

There is so much to learn about Me. My Spirit is multi-faceted, and it will take eternity to see and understand all that I AM. However, now is the time to begin. I am waiting to unfold the mysteries of My Kingdom to you.

Does not My Word say, Seek you first the kingdom of God and His righteousness and all these things shall be added unto you?[2] Your priorities have to be in order—My order!

Remember that My thoughts are not your thoughts, nor are your ways My ways. For as the heavens are higher than the earth, so are My ways higher than your ways, and My thoughts your thoughts.[3] I operate out of My heart of love for you and this is what you must believe.

I am the faithful great I AM! There is no shadow of turning in Me. Since I spoke, 'LET THERE BE LIGHT' and breathed life into Adam, I have demonstrated My faithfulness.

Did I not take righteous Noah and save his family because I knew his heart? He found grace in My eyes. When I gave him instructions of how to build the ark, he did according to all that I commanded him to do.

So, My precious ones, as you choose to continue the journey, know that I will be with you. The key for you is obedience. You must be willing to continually lay aside anything that would interfere with our relationship. You will never walk alone.

There are many old hymns written about the Holy Spirit as well as many contemporary songs. The anointing comes on the songs—whether old or new—when our hearts cry out, "Holy Spirit, fall afresh on me, until my will is lost in Yours and my desire is to live for You alone." Thank You, Lord for the joy of being Your child.

OUR PRAYER AND RESPONSE

Abba Father, I know that you have prepared me for such a time as this. I will accept the call that You have for me. Yes, I will come and take my place. Thank You for the enlightenment that will come as we continue this journey together. As I open another door, hand me the keys to unlock the wonderful facets of Holy Spirit.

Chapter 5

The Spirits Of Wisdom And Understanding

Wisdom is the principal thing; Therefore, get wisdom, And in all your getting, get understanding.

Proverbs 4:7

AM Wisdom! The wisdom of man is foolishness to Me. Do I not sit and laugh at the wicked as they take counsel together, against Me and against My anointed ones? Allow Me to open the eyes of your heart. I will show you a more accurate understanding of wisdom and understanding.

My heart's cry is that My people would ask to be filled with the Spirit of wisdom and revelation in the knowledge of Me. The path to intimacy is a journey throughout eternity. However, the day of your coming to Me as Lord is the time to begin. Your first desire must be to know Me. Then out of the depths of our relationship, you will continue to grow in the attributes of Holy Spirit.

The wisdom that comes from My Spirit is pure and undefiled by the world. Such wisdom involves knowing My truth and how to apply it in any given situation. You can have the wisdom of the world and walk in complete ignorance of My ways.

Harshness often comes from those that grab hold of a truth but never allow the truth to be seasoned with My love. That is why Word and Spirit must go hand in hand.

The Spirit of Understanding reveals My supernatural revelation. As you read My Word, the Spirit of Understanding gives you My secret insights, which are mysteries that cannot be uncovered with the natural mind. Ask of Me and I will show you how to understand the ways of My precepts. My Word says, "Through wisdom a house is built and by understanding it is established."[1]

Often when you think of wisdom, you think of Solomon. Yes, I gave Solomon My wisdom—exceedingly great understanding and largeness of heart like the sand on the seashore. Thus, his wisdom excelled beyond the wisdom of all the men of the East and all the wisdom of Egypt. He was wiser than all men.

At the end of his life, Solomon departed from My ways. What grief his actions were to My heart! My wisdom was no longer a guiding force in his life.

He made the choice to walk in disobedience and no longer obeyed my commandments. He loved many foreign women, as well as the daughter of Pharaoh; women of the Moabites, Ammonites, Edomites, Sidonians, and Hittites—from the nations of whom I had said to the children of Israel, "You shall not intermarry with them, nor they with you. Surely they will turn away your hearts after their gods." I watched as Solomon clung to these forbidden women he loved.

Listen carefully now, as I point out to you the two things that caused Solomon's downfall. First of all, he never walked in true intimacy with Me, as did his father, David. Then he chose to walk in disobedience. Yes, he had great wisdom, but it was not saturated with My love.

One of the key commandments he wrote but failed to obey himself was this—"Trust in the Lord with all your heart, and lean not on your own understanding. In all your ways acknowledge Him and He shall direct your steps."[2]

I hear your thoughts, My children. You might say, "Lord, I would never walk in disobedience as Solomon did." Truly your actions may be different but all human hearts are capable of rebellion. That is why total obedience and not partial obedience is mandatory. It is out of great love for you that I require boundaries.

My boundaries are necessary because what happens outside of My Presence easily becomes an abuse of power. Solomon was king and full of wisdom, but he became his own god. His lustful desires became a major stronghold and ruled his decisions.

Listen carefully as I speak to you with a father's heart. I love you with a love unspeakable, desiring above all else that you fulfill your destiny. Trust Me that I alone know what will bring you true joy. This is not the happy-go-lucky sort of joy that the world embraces. This is a deep heartfelt joy that rises above the circumstances and trials of everyday life.

Ask this day to be flooded afresh with the Spirit of Wisdom and the Spirit of Understanding. Do not forget, nor turn away from the words of My mouth. As you ask of Me, I will impart these truths into your heart.

As you come into an even greater awareness of Who I AM, every facet of My being will shine forth like a beautiful diamond, which with the naked eye you only see the overall beauty of the stone. However, as the jeweler puts the jewel under the magnifying glass, every small characteristic can be examined and appreciated.

There will never be a point in time that you will fully arrive. However, walking with Me is like being in a field filled with treasure. There is always something new and wonderful to uncover and embrace. My wisdom is the sum of learning through the ages—encompassing the ability to discern or judge what is true, right, and lasting.

As you read and meditate on these scriptures, allow Me to inscribe them on your heart.

> *Oh, My children, the depth of the riches both*
> *Of My wisdom and knowledge.*
> *How unsearchable are My judgments*
> *And My Ways are past finding out!*
> *Who has known My mind?*
> *Or who has become My counselor?*
> *Or who has first given to Me and it shall be*
> *repaid to him?* [3]

❖ ❖ ❖

OUR PRAYER AND RESPONSE

Yes, Lord for of You and through You and to You are all things, and to You be glory forever. Father God, we know that throughout eternity we will continue to discover the depth of Your wisdom and revelation. However, the most exciting part is to know that now is the time to begin. You are visiting us and calling our names. We are saying, 'Yes, Lord,' and running to embrace You as we open another door.

Chapter 6

The Spirits Of Counsel And Might

*You are great in counsel and mighty in work,
for your eyes are open to all the ways of the sons
of men to give everyone according to his ways
and according to the fruit of his doings.*

Jeremiah 32:19

As the Judge of all the earth, will I not do what is right? I have promised that I would never leave you as orphans. In My heavenly court, you have representation. The enemy of your soul desires to condemn you. He looks for every opportunity to draw you away from My purposes. However, the Spirit of Counsel is there to plead your case. He opens your book and sees the blood of Jesus covering your sins. At the end of time, My gavel will go down and I will declare—not guilty.

The angels are declaring, "Listen carefully—I AM that I AM—is making a decree!" Everything that is needed for you to walk successfully in My Kingdom is already in place. My called-out ones, allow Me to fill you to overflowing with the Spirit of Counsel and the Spirit of Might.

The Spirit of Counsel will be your personal advisor, helper and guide. Yes, I am at work in you both to will and to do for My good pleasure. As you continue to seek My heart, I will give you the desire and ability to do what pleases Me.

You must know that this is the hour that I am drawing those apart that are seeking first the Kingdom of God. As you are willing to lay aside your agenda, the Spirit of Counsel will give you a clearer understanding of My ways.

Many of the people that call themselves by My name run here and there, seeking counsel and advice in all the wrong places. Often the counsel that they receive does not line up with My Word. In fact, it often contradicts what I have declared to be My will and My heart.

They justify accepting this counsel because they say, "Is not counsel supposed to be an exchange of opinions and ideas in order to reach a decision? Therefore, I have the right to state my thoughts and opinions about a situation. Then I will decide what I want to do." However, don't you see, this is the very thing that began in the garden with the apple?

No, I did not make you to be robots. If you know Me intimately, such a thought would never cross your mind. I am greatly pleased when My children excel in what I have called them to do. I must ask you: Is the desire of your heart to do My will?

My Word explicitly says that I will guide you with My counsel. However, you have a choice. Do you want the counsel of My will, which signifies My eternal and unchangeable plan?

Many of My children have no clue why I have put them on earth. They may know the vocation that they want to pursue. One woman's heart desire is to get married and raise a family. Another woman's desire may be to become a doctor. A young man may be planning to go to law school. None of these desires or choices is wrong. However, many never stop to ask, "Lord, what is Your plan for me? What is my purpose for being here?"

If you will take time to sit in My Presence, My purpose and plan for you will begin to unfold. As you listen to My voice, I will instruct you and teach you in the way that you should go. I will guide you, keeping My eye upon you.

My will was never for My people to just exist. Too many accept Me as Lord and Savior but then just go on with their lives independent of Me. If only they would allow the Spirit of Counsel to give them instruction and direction, they could experience great joy by seeing their lives through the eyes of Holy Spirit. The natural man cannot understand the things of the Spirit, for they are foolishness to him, because they must be spiritually discerned.

The Spirit of Counsel and the Spirit of Might serve as protectors for My people. Too many want My power but not My counsel. Walking in intimacy causes one to increase in understanding of the manifold purposes of Holy Spirit. Jesus commanded His disciples and He is challenging you to: walk in My power and My authority.

As My son or daughter, you should desire to see the lame walk, the blind see and the deaf hear. Now is the time to cry out for the lost and hurting. Open your eyes to see the great need for miracles that produce changed lives.

There are no words to adequately describe My power. It is as My Word says—immeasurable. However, there must be a blending of the Spirits of Counsel and Might. There are times that My people have prayed and seen tornados change direction and storms dissipate. On other occasions, My plan is not for a storm to be calmed. The key is acquiring My counsel on how to pray and taking time to seek My heart.

In My Presence, you learn to trust. I am a God of love. However, there are some things that you may not understand this side of heaven. Trust does not develop overnight. It is sown as a small seed, then watered and cared for in My Presence. The day must come when you do not doubt My love, no matter what the circumstances appear to be.

My precious ones, I will never leave you or forsake you. There is no shadow of turning in Me. Yes, I am the same yesterday, today and forever. The Spirit of Counsel will continue to instruct and teach you and the Spirit of Might will hold back the gates of hell that prevail against you.

Abba Father reveals mysteries to those that love Him and seek His face. Now allow Him to instill in you the counsel of His greatness and might. After all, we do serve a Mighty God!

❖ ❖ ❖

OUR PRAYER AND RESPONSE

Precious Lord, You are the Mighty Counselor! Your caring heart has been imparted to us as we have lingered in Your Presence. As the Spirits of Counsel and Might have become a reality in our lives, we are better equipped to be what You have commissioned us to be. Knowing in this season You are visiting Your people, we will continue to seek Your face. Opening the next door will cause us to hear Your voice as You teach us about the Spirit of Knowledge. THANK YOU, ABBA FATHER.

Chapter 7

The Spirit Of Knowledge

Talk no more so very proudly,
Let no arrogance come from your mouth.
For the Lord is the God of knowledge:
And by Him actions are weighed.

1 Samuel 2:3

I AM the God of knowledge. By Me the thoughts and actions of all mankind are weighed. So do not be ignorant of My ways. As you ask of Me, I will give you great insight of things, which were previously hidden. Only My Spirit can uncover such mysteries.

In this hour, My eyes are roaming across the earth looking for those that I can trust. I am seeking people whose hearts are loyal to Me. I desire to endue them with My power and a greater knowledge of Me.

I am calling forth those that yearn for Me above all else. Their hearts will crave knowledge of Me more than silver or gold.

So many seemingly good deeds are done with wrong motives. That is why I encourage you to pray as David prayed, "Search Me, O God, and know My heart, try me and know My anxieties and see if there be any wicked way in me and lead me in the way everlasting."[1]

The pull of the world is so strong on some of you that you cannot even hear Me calling. This is a time for My visitation. I am patient and will wait. However, there is a season for all things; and when that season passes, I will wait no longer. Oh, yes, you will have eternity with Me, but I will woo you no longer. Now is the time to seek My face.

As the Scriptures tell you, My Son wept over Jerusalem. He said to them, "If you had known, even you, especially in this your day, the things that make for your peace! But now they are hidden from your eyes. Much of this is because you did not know the time of your visitation."[2]

Of course, My Son was referring to His visitation on earth and their failing to recognize and accept Who He was. However, as I have told you, I am visiting My children in this hour to call them up to a higher place. In order for them to accomplish all that I have called them to do, they must know Me intimately. As they continue to draw aside with Me, I will pour into them My exceedingly great power and grace.

Throughout Scripture, I warn My people. 'Hear the word of the Lord, you children of Israel, for I am bringing a charge against the inhabitants of the land. There is no truth or mercy or knowledge of God in the land. I do not see as man sees: for man looks at the outward appearance but I look at the heart.'[3]

Often My people honor Me with their mouths but their hearts are far from Me. They choose to reject the knowledge of Me and are filled with the pride of life.

Yes, My Word tells you that My people have gone into captivity because they have no knowledge. Listen carefully; there are all kinds of captivity. That is why you must seek Me first before you are captured by something that could enslave you. Remember, as you seek Me first, all other things will be added unto you.

As knowledge of Me increases, clear direction for your life will be revealed. I will speak words of knowledge that will be the key to open another door. These words will not be just for you but given that you might bring life to others.

The Spirit of Knowledge imparts a greater discernment of those matters that you may not understand. You will be able to distinguish between what is of Me and what is of your flesh. It is often not a choice between good and evil. The key that unlocks the door is what My will is for you in each situation.

I am able to make a way where there seems to be no way. However, you must be willing to continue down the path to open the next door. Also, when I say stop and tarry here with Me, you must put aside your agenda and wait with Me.

As you come into My Presence, I will impart more and more of My anointing. I will perfect that which concerns you. My Presence will go before you, rest upon you and follow after you.

I want you to stop for a moment—visualize you and Me walking together down a path. How far are you willing to go? Are you willing to do and say only the things that you hear Me say and do? Remember when Jesus walked on the earth, He could only do the things that He saw Me do? Are you willing to do the same?

OUR PRAYER AND RESPONSE

Precious Lord, our heart's cry is that we might desire to seek You with all our hearts. There is no greater purpose than knowing You. Thank You for the Spirit of Knowledge. You are supplying us with what is needed in this hour to rise above circumstances and truly think like You think. We love You and are excited about the next step on our walk with You.

One thing I have desired of You, Lord
That will I seek:
That I may dwell in Your house
All the days of my life,
To behold Your beauty
And to inquire in Your temple. [4]

Chapter 8

The Spirit Of The Fear Of The Lord

The fear of the Lord is the beginning of wisdom;
A good understanding have all those who do
His commandments. His praise endures forever.

Psalms 111:10

ear of Me is truly the beginning of all wisdom and knowledge. This is what I require of you—to fear Me, to walk in all of My ways and to love Me with all your heart, soul and mind. Yes, it is My command that you serve Me in total obedience.

My Son loved to teach in parables when He was on the earth as a man. So listen with your spiritual ears as I relate this story. It portrays My heart as well as the battle of not understanding the requirement to fear Me.

As I waited patiently outside the door, I heard this argument going on: A man that we will call Ray was venting with a friend,

"Why would a good God want me to fear Him? That doesn't make sense to me. I think that this is a door that I will leave closed. After all, I have already come a long way on this journey. What more will He expect of me?"

The story progresses as Ray finds himself in the midst of a major crisis at work. People are being laid off. Those that keep their jobs, find that their salaries and hours have been cut. Ray feels fear like he has never felt it before. What will he do? He has three children and a wife to feed, clothe and educate.

This is the time that I chose to speak to him in My still small voice, "Ray, you are fearing the wrong thing? I have promised you that I would take care of you. Open this door and let Me show you why fear of Me is so important."

As he drove home that night, Ray called out to Me saying, "I believe, but please Lord help my unbelief. I need the grace to trust You. Please give me understanding as I open this door."

I responded as he walked through the door, "My son, you will not regret this decision. Now come and sit down with Me as I quiet your fears and give you My peace. I am calling you to serve Me in sincerity and truth. Therefore, it is good that you were transparent with your struggles concerning fear of Me. Now I will teach you and soon you will see that it is a very good thing."

The struggle over having a reverent fear of Me began with satan. If satan had feared Me, pride would have had no place to take root. When pride and arrogance took over his whole being, there was nothing to stop him from desiring to be equal or superior to Me. He could see nothing but how wonderful he was.

A person that has a true fear of Me is like a teenager with a healthy fear of their parents. Children will obey out of fear of punishment if rules are broken, but their fear is actually a safety net protecting them.

To walk in the fear of Me, you must be willing to lose your life. Your desire must be totally immersed in the reality of My will for you.

Yes, the fear of Me involves complete surrender to whatever I have for you. Your heart must cry out in sincerity, "Your will, Lord, and not mine be done." Did not My Son set the perfect example of obedience?

Joshua had seen what happened to the children of Israel in the wilderness. The spies—except for Joshua and Caleb—walked in fear and unbelief. Their lack of trust in Me resulted in the children of Israel having to stay in the wilderness another forty years. Now under Joshua's leadership, they were in Canaan. Joshua knew that they had a choice to make. They must fear Me and serve Me with sincerity.

Joshua boldly declared: "Choose this day whom you will serve...However, be assured that as for me and my house, we will serve the Lord."[1]

You must understand that it is not enough to just fear Me. Therefore, you should not just pray for the fear of the Lord but for the SPIRIT OF THE FEAR OF THE LORD. He is a portion of Who I AM.

The Spirit of the Fear of the Lord upon you will be required to walk victoriously in the last days. Should you not fear Me?

Should you not tremble in My Presence? I made the sand and coral reefs and rocks as a barrier to contain the sea. The waves may roll, but they cannot prevail; they may roar, but they cannot cross the boundary I have put in place.

The Spirit of the Fear of the Lord empowers you to perform My Word. You are quickened to obey without hesitation—to activate immediate obedience. As you walk in this anointing, the things of this world will not attract you and pull you away from My plans and purposes.

So, My children, know that wisdom and knowledge shall be your stability and strength. The fear of Me shall be your treasure as I reveal My secrets to those who fear Me.

The fear of Me brings many promises—one of which is divine protection. Even if the enemy comes in like a flood, the Spirit of the Lord shall lift up a standard against him.

Don't forget, the world will get darker but you are not of this world. You live in the world but you are a part of My Kingdom, which is eternal. So you will have rest and be edified as you continue to walk in the fear of the Lord and the power of Holy Spirit.

Psalms 95 reveals the hardness, which can arise in the hearts of men. We must have the Spirit of the Fear of the Lord—to hear His voice and know His ways.

Oh come, let us sing to the Lord!
Let us shout joyfully to the Rock of our salvation.

Let us come before His Presence with thanksgiving;
Let us shout joyfully to Him with psalms.

For the Lord is the great God,
And the great King above all gods.

In His hand are the deep places of the earth:
The heights of the hills are His also.

The sea is His, for He made it;
And His hands formed the dry land.

Oh come, let us worship and bow down;
Let us kneel before the Lord our Maker.

For He is our God, And we are the people
of His pasture, And the sheep of His hand.

Today if you will hear His voice;
Do not harden your hearts, as in the rebellion,
As in the day of trial in the wilderness

When your fathers tested Me;
Tried Me, though they saw My work.

For forty years I was grieved with that generation,
And said, 'It is a people who go astray in their hearts.
And they do not know My ways.'
So I swore in My wrath,

They shall not enter My rest.

OUR PRAYER AND RESPONSE

Father God, we ask that You increase our understanding of the Spirit of the Fear of the Lord. Thank You for not giving up on us, even when we shrink back. By Your grace, we will continue on this the journey with You. We love You, Precious Lord.

Chapter 9

Lay Aside Every Weight

Therefore we also, since we are surrounded by so great a cloud of witnesses, let us lay aside every weight, and the sin which so easily ensnares us, and let us run with endurance the race that is set before us.

Hebrews 12:1

Is your foundation firmly in place? Why would you call Me, 'Lord, Lord,' and not do the things which I say? Whoever comes to Me and hears My sayings and does them will be like a man building a house, who dug deep and laid the foundation on the rock. And when the flood rose, the waters beat vehemently against that house and could not shake it, because it was founded on the Rock.

The entrance to the door of this house is very narrow. It requires laying down those things, which are not required for this part of your journey. They are not necessarily bad things, but they could cause you to stumble with the weight of them. Remember, My burden is easy and My yoke is light.

Do not look around you to see what others may be doing. There are people around you that you have known for a long time, and some of them will not choose to go through this door. Others will come, but they may not be required to lay aside the things that I have asked of you. Fasten your eyes on Me! Keep in mind that the fear of man brings a snare.

The doors that you have previously walked through have prepared you for what is ahead. The Spirit of the Lord has opened to you the understanding of the seven-fold Spirit of God. In the past you have been filled with Holy Spirit, but now you must embrace all that He has to give you.

The fullness of Holy Spirit shall rest upon you. Yes, the Spirit of the Lord, the Spirit of Wisdom, the Spirit of Understanding, the Spirit of Counsel, the Spirit of Might, the Spirit of Knowledge and the Spirit of the Fear of the Lord are yours for the asking.

Full understanding will come as you continue to allow Me to teach you all things. I will instruct you and I will guide you with My eye.

Now is the time to allow Me to pour the balm of Gilead deep into the crevices of your heart. The enemy cannot hold you back from your destiny. You may have been disappointed in the past because you did not understand My eternal perspective. Know that I am healing hope deferred in your life, so let go and receive My precious balm.

You must forgive those that have hurt you and release yesterday's pains to Me. Yes, I understand that it is very difficult.

However, the only way that you will be able to receive My total peace is to let go of past traumas. My Son is the perfect example of forgiveness. While on the cross, He cried out, "Forgive them, Father, they know not what they do."[1]

My children, listen very carefully! Some of you must let go of your hidden anger towards Me. You have buried this pain because you were afraid to admit that you were disappointed in Me. Until you let go of this anger, you will not be able to embrace the complete fullness of My Spirit.

Settle your mind that there are just some things you will never completely understand in this life. That is where your love and trust in Me has to come up to a new dimension.

Just cry out to Me and let Me embrace you. Believe Me when I tell you that I was weeping with you. Now is the time and the hour for total healing.

Never forget that what the enemy meant for evil, I will cause to work together for good.

I have brought you to a new comprehension of the Spirit of the Fear of the Lord. You must embrace this truth with your whole heart. Without grasping this facet of My Spirit, you will find it very difficult, if not impossible, to continue your journey into the intimacy of My presence.

People that do not understand your walk with Me may criticize you, and others may think you have gone off the deep end. However, you cannot bow your knee to their opinions.

So, remember the words written by Paul in My Word; "I press on, that I may lay hold of that for which Christ Jesus has also laid hold of me. I do not count myself to have apprehended; but one thing I do, forgetting those things which are behind and reaching forward to those things which are ahead."[2]

When storms rage about us, our only hope is in Your glory. Worship lights the way for us to overcome and experience victory as we set our eyes on You and You alone:

HOPE OF GLORY

You are my hope of glory, my shelter from the storm.
I lift my eyes up to You, the shelter safe and warm.
You are the hope of glory, the light of a new day for me.
So I will worship You until You see me through.

You are my hope of glory; You are my shining light,
My calm in the raging storm.
You are my hope of glory, a safe haven for me.
So I fix my eyes on You.

You are my hope of glory, You are my victory story.
You are my harbor in the storm and
You are my light in the darkness.
You are the shelter for me and
You are the God who leads me on.[3]

❖ ❖ ❖

OUR PRAYER AND RESPONSE

Lord, I ask You to convict my heart. What is Your request? I will be obedient and lay it down. I will not allow anything to hold me back from what You have destined for this hour. Please, Lord, fill me afresh with Your Spirit. Yes, I want to be filled with all that entails—the Spirit of the Lord, the Spirits of Wisdom and Understanding, the Spirits of Counsel and Might, the Spirit of Knowledge and the Spirit of the Fear of the Lord. I commit to going all the way with You!

I love You, Lord.

Chapter 10

Seated In Heavenly Places

*But God, who is rich in mercy, because of His
great love with which He loved us, even when
we were dead in trespasses, made us alive together with Christ (by grace you have been saved),
and raised us up together, and made us sit
together in the heavenly places in Christ Jesus.*

Ephesians 2:4-6

My children, as another door opens, do not allow yourselves to be distracted. What I am sharing— many of you have heard or read from the scriptures for years. However, you may not have grabbed hold of the total truth. I have called you to sit in heavenly places with Me.

Even before the fall of man in the garden, I had a plan. The major part of that plan was the CROSS. Jesus paid the ultimate price, and you are free because He shed His blood. Please allow Me to burn this into your heart—heavenly power begins now, not when you die. You must begin to see things from an eternal perspective.

Jesus is seated at My right hand in the heavens, and He rules with all authority. Satan has been defeated. However, you must see yourself seated in heavenly places as well. I have given you all authority by the blood of Jesus. Whatever I ask you to do, you can accomplish through the name and the blood of My SON.

My Son broke the chains of satan's authority at the cross. However, you are in a war because the enemy of your soul continues to fight against you. Satan's purpose is to cause you to sin, which will open up a hole in your armor. The good news is that you can always repent and turn from your sin. I cover those holes with His Precious Blood.

The prayer that you know as *THE LORD'S PRAYER* says, "Thy will be done on earth as it is in heaven." What you are declaring as you say this prayer is: "Father, it is possible for Your will to be duplicated on earth, just like it has already been done in heaven." As you are seated in heavenly places, I am showing you things from My perspective.

If you fail to understand this truth, you will never walk in total victory. Truly seeing yourself seated in heavenly places will cause you to be heavenly minded in a good way. It was the enemy of your soul that came up with this false statement—they are so heavenly minded that they are no earthly good. Satan wants you bound to the things of this world.

The good news is—when you grasp the truth of My Kingdom on earth—then My power flows through you like a faucet.

Remember the truth of My Word—Jesus said all power was given unto you, as well as all authority.

The key to victory is fulfilling your assignment. When I call, you must declare that the power and authority is there for you to finish the race. A declaration is not just giving lip service to what you think you should believe. It is a faith statement that what is declared on earth has already been established in heaven.

Unless you have been spending time with Me in the secret place, you cannot understand that what I am sharing with you must be grasped with your spirit. The natural man cannot comprehend the things of the Spirit.

This is the time that I am visiting My people, and now is the time to truly seek My face. Start from where you are and commit to Me your lack of understanding. I will illuminate My truth to you.

You were created with a void that only I can fill. Some of you have been walking with Me for a long time. However, you are feeling discontent and dissatisfied, because you have failed to put aside those things that are hindering your walk with Me. Some of you are caught up in religion, which leaves no place for the things of the Spirit.

Wherever you are in your walk with Me, don't stop. There is more to come. More doors are in front of you to open, and there are more people to reach.

Run with Me. The race is on and the prize is waiting. There is no greater prize than the joy that we can have together now and throughout eternity.

OUR PRAYER AND RESPONSE

Father God, we thank You that by faith we are seated in heavenly places with You. There is no way that we can understand this truth with our natural minds. That is why we must thank You that the eyes of our understanding will be enlightened to know what is the hope of Your calling for us. It is by the power of the Holy Spirit and the blood of Jesus that we are enabled to be seated in heavenly places. We thank You for greater revelation. Believing that You will teach us step-by-step and precept-upon-precept, we give You praise.

Chapter 11

Come Up Here

After these things I looked, and behold, a door standing open in heaven. And the first voice which I heard was like a trumpet speaking with me, saying, "Come up here, and I will show you things which must take place after this.

Revelations 4:1

As you continue to walk with Me, many of you will have heavenly encounters. Some of you will see angels and do exploits. The key to entering into or operating in the heavenly realm is total obedience. It is imperative as well that the Spirit of the Fear of the Lord be upon you.

Some of My leaders in the past have gone astray because they failed to walk in obedience. They desired the things of My Spirit. However, their heart's desire was to use this knowledge to draw people to themselves. They sought to be elevated in the eyes of man.

John, My beloved disciple, was one that I could trust with all things. He never asked, "Lord, why do I have to go through all of this? I do not like being exiled on the island of Patmos." It was a joy for Me to reveal My deepest secrets to him. I knew that he could be trusted.

Listen to Me now as we recall John's experience. He saw a door standing open in heaven and heard the voice of Jesus summoning him to come up to the throne room.

When I brought him up into My throne room, His eyes were bright with joy and adoration. He stood in awe of ME.

Jesus summoned him in order that John might receive a heavenly perspective of things, which must take place on the earth.

An important fact to remember is that I never do anything on earth without first revealing it to my prophets. Therefore, My people who are listening will not be caught off guard.

The first thing that John saw was My throne set in heaven. He saw Me sitting on the throne. John could not adequately describe My appearance—all He could see was the beauty that covered Me.

From My throne proceeded lightning, thunder, and voices. Seven lamps of fire were burning before the throne, which are the seven Spirits of God.

Remember, My children, we have already talked about the seven Spirits of God. It is crucial that you let Me burn into your hearts the necessity of the fullness of My Spirit.

You have now entered by faith—the open door into My throne room. Join the four living creatures as they sing;

> *Holy, holy, holy*
> *Lord God almighty,*
> *Who was and is and is to come[1]…*

I watched John that day as he walked around the throne room. His eyes were bright with excitement and wonders of all that He was observing.

John joined the twenty-four elders as they fell down before Me. He saw the crowns as they were cast before the throne. His voice rang out with joy as the elders said: "You are worthy, O Lord, to receive glory and honor and power; for You created all things, and by Your will they exist and were created."[2]

Throughout the ages, there have been people like John that have observed the wonders of the throne room. The apostle Paul shares his experience of being caught up to the third heaven, Paradise, where he heard inexpressible words. Paul made it very clear that he would not be boastful about his experiences or what he saw there.

My heart's desire is to have a people that are united for one purpose—to seek My face and do My will. Then trust must come—understanding that I AM will give them what they need to finish the race.

If you are parents or grandparents, you know what a joy it is to share all that you are and have with your family. You would never think of hiding a family treasure to keep it just for your-self. However, many see Me as a god that only wants to be feared and worshipped. They think of fear and worship in a negative way. Then when a tragedy comes, they ask, "Why would anyone want to serve a god that allows a young father to die with cancer?" My ways and purposes cannot be discerned by the human mind.

Truly, it is with great joy that I want to show you everything that is part of your inheritance. I have called you to reign with Me throughout eternity. Many question and wonder what it will be like to live forever and ever. I gave John—as I have given some of you—just a foretaste of all that I have for you.

Some of you are seeking Me with all your hearts. You may be asking yourself, "Lord, why do some people have heavenly encounters and others don't?" If you are not careful, such desire can become a jealousy factor. My children, I am jealous over you because I want you protected from the evil one.

Seek Me with all your heart, and I promise that you will not be disappointed. My ways may not always be as you think they should be—but remember you must trust Me with all your heart. I alone know what is best for you.

John, also, saw Jesus portrayed as the Lamb, the only One worthy to take the scroll out of My hand and open its seals. The Lamb redeemed you by His blood. Therefore He has made you kings and priests to reign on the earth.

It is important that you learn and understand the song of the Lamb. The truth of it needs to penetrate deep into your hearts:

Worthy is the Lamb who was slain
To receive power and riches and wisdom
And strength and honor and glory and blessing.[3]

As these words penetrate your hearts, know that as the Lamb received from Me so He has given to each of you. There is an abundance of all that is needed to fulfill your place in My Kingdom. There is no lack. Now receive by faith that which is needed to finish the race.

❖ ❖ ❖

OUR PRAYER AND RESPONSE

Oh, precious Father we declare that at the name of Jesus every knee should bow, of those in heaven, and those on the earth, and those under the earth. We shall proclaim together:

Blessings and honor and glory and power
Be to Him who sits on the throne
And to the Lamb, forever and ever![4]
Amen and Amen.

Chapter 12

Carriers Of His Presence

*God be merciful to us and bless us
And cause your face to shine upon us.*

Psalms 67:1

yearn for a people who desire to be Carriers of My Presence. After spending time with Me in the secret place, the glow of My Spirit will shine on their faces. The anointing of My Presence upon them will draw others into My Kingdom.

The glow of My anointing is like glue, joining spirit-to-spirit. This is a supernatural love that cannot be counterfeited by human concern. My love is unconditional and looks beyond the sins and flaws in a person's life. It is impossible to fake that kind of supernatural love and care.

When My Son encountered the woman at the well, He did not condemn her. Rather, the power of Holy Spirit in Him gently convicted her. He, a Jewish man, was not ashamed to ask a Samaritan woman for a drink. His confidence was not in what others thought of Him, because His desire was always to do My will.

My Word tells the story of the men who caught the woman in adultery and immediately brought her to Jesus. They tested Him that they might have something of which to accuse Him. With great wisdom My Son looked those men in the eye and said, "He that is without sin, cast the first stone."[1] One by one they walked away. These men knew the Scriptures but they did not know Me.

Jesus asked the woman, "Where are your accusers? Has no one condemned you?"[2] She replied, "No one, Lord." Jesus said to her, "Neither do I condemn you; go and sin no more."[3]

My Son spoke just as I am speaking with you now. "I am the light of the world, he who follows Me shall not walk in darkness but have the light of life."[4]

Come aside with Me for a moment and I will give you a glimpse of one of My PRESENCE CARRIERS.

Her name is Georgia. She and her husband were missionaries in Africa for many years. In that land they buried two of their precious babies. When it came time for them to return to America, the fruit of their labor could not be seen with the naked eye. However, the eternal reward that was theirs to receive at the end of time was not hidden from Me.

A group of young ladies are gathered around Georgia, listening intently as she speaks. One of the ladies—who is listening with her heart—senses that Miss Georgia, as they call her, is not your average Bible teacher. This young lady goes home eternally changed. She has experienced the reality of truly being in My Presence.

Stephen, one of the seven deacons, was a PRESENCE CARRIER. He was a man, full of faith and great power. His listeners were not able to resist the wisdom and Spirit by which he spoke. However, his enemies secretly induced men to speak out against him.

When Stephen was brought to the synagogue council to be questioned, all who sat there saw his face as the face of an angel. After hearing him speak, they were cut to the heart and gnashed at him with their teeth.

But Stephen, being full of the Holy Spirit gazed into heaven and saw My Glory and Jesus standing at My right side. Then as the religious leaders were stoning him, he cried out with a loud voice, "Father, do not charge them with this sin."[5]

My children unfortunately have often been seen as weak and powerless. Those outside My family see nothing in them that they desire. Actually, looking from the outside there is nothing that sets them apart. Everyone just flows and mingles together. Many of My sons and daughters have forgotten that My Word says that they are not to be conformed to this world, but be transformed by the renewing of their minds, that they may prove what is My good and acceptable will.[6]

My will is that all who believe will be full of great grace that flows out of them with great power. They will be world changers and shine as lights in a dark place.

All are not willing to pay the price to be part of My Triumphant Reserve. I am calling you. Will you respond and say, "Abba Father, all that I am and will ever be, I give to You. I desire to be a PRESENCE CARRIER—to be Your light in the midst of the darkness?"

With this commitment you and I will co-labor together, and you will continue to learn from Me. By the power of Holy Spirit I will teach you what is needed in this hour.

❖ ❖ ❖

OUR PRAYER AND RESPONSE

Father God, as our understanding of You increases, it causes us to yearn even more for Your Presence. What a joy to know that throughout eternity we will be with You.

Thank You for being our Teacher, Guide and Director. We desire to be Presence Carriers—Your lights in the midst of darkness. How thankful we are that You have given all power and grace to sustain us.

We adore You, Lord.

Chapter 13

The Glory Realm

*Arise; shine; for your light has come! And the
glory of the Lord is risen upon you. For behold
the darkness shall cover the earth and deep darkness the people, but the Lord will arise over you
and His glory will be seen upon you.*

Isaiah 60:1-2

*S*cripture clearly states that a time will come when great
darkness will cover the earth. Even in this present season, you are seeing a foreboding increase in spiritual
darkness. However, do not be distracted by the enemy's plans
for destruction. Instead, look to Me to hear what I am saying in
this hour.

Jesus glorified Me on the earth. He did this by finishing the
work, which I had given Him to do. First He died daily to what
He, as a man, wanted to do; because His heart was totally committed to only do what He saw Me doing. Then He died on the
cross, which was the Ultimate Sacrifice.

I deeply desire to have a people through whom I can display My glory. What a delight it would be if each one of My children would live a life that is fully overshadowed by My glory. This manifestation will come to those that seek Me and welcome My Presence in their midst—privately and corporately. If you truly seek Me with all your heart, you will find Me.

There will be a remnant—The Triumphant Reserve. They will not be content with anything less than a full-scale revival of My glory, covering the earth as the waters cover the sea.

There are many descriptions given by those who have physically experienced My glory. Some have testified that the "Glory Realm" is like being surrounded by a heavy presence, like a blanket of warmth and peace settling over them. It is often seen as a 'golden mist.'

Holy Spirit is working in the hearts of My children that are hungry for an even closer relationship with Me. He is shifting their vision towards a commitment to the full understanding of the "Glory Realm."

The prayer that Jesus lifted up was, "That the love with which You loved Me may be in them."[1] His desire was to bring My people into the intimate experience of My love. This is the ultimate glory encounter.

My precious Ones, we have talked about John entering heaven and what he experienced. You also are invited to experientially enter the Most Holy Place that is filled with the shekinah glory of God. You must have confidence to enter the Most Holy Place by the blood of Jesus. Then draw near to Me with a sincere heart in full assurance of faith.

Jesus trained His disciples to do the same miraculous works that He did. So are My committed Ones called to be the releasers of the glory realm of heaven. The words that Holy Spirit will speak through you will be full of great power to even recreate matter at the quantum level.

Jesus trusted Me even when He had to walk through the valley of the shadow of death in the Garden of Gethsemane. His faith did not waver, because He was secure in My love.

Just as I commanded light to shine out of darkness, I have shone in your hearts to give you the light of the knowledge of My glory in the face of Jesus Christ. I am calling you to keep your eyes steadily on His face. As you have this face-to-face encounter, an inward transformation will take place within you.

I desire to grip My people with the reality of heaven and the unlimited power that can be unleashed through a radically set-apart life.

The knowledge of My glory is the pathway to moving in creative miracles. This is a prize worth laying aside every distraction to pursue. May your declaration be as the apostle Paul's: "I press toward the goal for the prize of the upward call of God in Christ Jesus."[2]

Therefore, My children, it is the time to arise and shine for your light is come. My glory has risen upon you. Yes, the darkness shall cover the earth, and deep darkness the people. But I will arise over you, and My glory will be seen upon you.

OUR PRAYER AND RESPONSE

Abba Father, we will press toward the goal of the upward call of God in Christ Jesus. Yes, we will arise and shine for our light has come. We know that there is so much more to learn and to understand! You are an awesome God! Thank You for loving us too much to leave us where we are. We know that we cannot fully understand the "Glory Realm" with our natural understanding. This knowledge has to be imparted by Holy Spirit. Thank You for taking us on this journey that never ends. All praise, glory and honor be to You, precious Lord.

Chapter 14

Majesty

*Splendor and majesty are before Him, strength
and beauty are in His sanctuary.*

Psalms 96:6

y Son willingly left the beauty of the throne room
and came to earth as a man. He humbled Himself
and was obedient to accept a horrific death on the
cross for you.

Therefore I have highly exalted Him and given Him the
name, which is above every name. Yes, the day will come "that at
the name of Jesus every knee will bow, of those in heaven, and of
those on earth, and of those under the earth."[1]

There will be—at the end of time—a coronation so magnif-
icent that it can only be described by the Spirit. No human can
adequately put in words the beauty of My Son's holiness.

Jesus will be crowned as King, but He is also a Warrior. At
a predestined hour in time, He will appear out of heaven riding

a white horse. He will be called Faithful and True. In righteousness, My Son will judge and make war.

Throughout the ages, many books have been written about the timing and sequence of the times of the end. I AM is the only one that knows the answer.

Too much time has been wasted arguing about the details of the rapture and tribulation. My heart in these days is for My people to seek My face. As they enter into My presence, they will be prepared for all that is to come.

When Jesus left the earth realm after His death, resurrection and ascension; He was given the place of honor at My right hand. I declared to Him that the day would come when all His enemies would be His footstool.

Through the years I have heard the cries of My Son as He interceded for you. His powerful voice was full of majesty as His heart cried out to you saying, "My friends, lay down anything that would cause you to stumble in your walk with Me. Come and I will show you My way. In Me and Me alone you will find peace. The answers that you are looking for will be found only by abiding in Me." The day will come that I will show you the battles that were won because of His intercession for you.

One of the truths that I desire to burn within you is that Jesus made it possible—through His death and resurrection—for you to do greater things. Remember, He told His disciples that they would do greater things than He had done. I am calling you in this hour to rise up and do even greater exploits.

You must continue to let the truth of the Gospels—Matthew, Mark, Luke and John—burn within you. The authors of these books were inspired by the Holy Spirit to portray the life of Jesus in the way that I want you to see Him. You must allow Me to show you the humanity of My Son. His body was flesh and blood just like yours. He was, at times, hungry, tired and sorrowful. Many tears were shed in His times of prayer on the mountain, as He reflected on the doubt and unbelief that filled the hearts of many of the religious leaders.

The truth is that on earth Jesus was all God and all man. He voluntarily limited Himself, but He gained strength and power by the Holy Spirit and exercised total abandonment to My will.

Human royalty does not have to go through the humiliation that My Son experienced. Their lives are filled with luxury and, yes, even with excess. However, no king or queen has ever received the glory, honor and power that will be given to Jesus.

On His robe will be written ***King of kings and Lord of lords***. He and He alone is worthy to receive all glory, honor and power. Yes, worthy is the Lamb who was slain to receive power and riches and wisdom and strength and honor and glory and blessings. So, My children, celebrate with Me for the day will come when My Son will be lifted up in all His Majesty.

Father, we rejoice with You. As we meditate on or sing the words of this hymn, we lift our voices to give You praise:

All hail the power of Jesus' name!
Let angels prostrate fall;
Bring forth the royal diadem,
And crown Him
LORD OF ALL!²

OUR PRAYER AND RESPONSE

Yes, Father, Yours is the greatness, the power and the glory, the victory and the majesty. All that is in the heavens is Yours, and You will reign throughout eternity. Thank you for the honor of being Your child. I persistently yield to You, Precious Abba, and ask for continual preparation for the joy of co-laboring with You.

Epilogue

*P*reviously, the Father gave you a glimpse of Miss Georgia's Ladies' Bible Study. The young lady that was eternally changed by sensing His Presence upon Miss Georgia was me.

Many years have passed since that morning in her home. I am still on the journey, seeking His heart and His will. I was forever spoiled once I tasted the fruit of His Spirit—love, peace, joy and kindness—that flowed from her that day. Even though she was naturally a precious lady, I knew this outpouring was so much more.

As we have walked together with the Lord through one door after another in this book, we have partaken of the depths of His heart. He has shared valuable truths and insights with us as He gently wooed us into His secret place.

May we continue to:

> *Dwell in the secret place of the Most High.*
> *And abide under the shadow of the Almighty.*
> *Yes, we shall say to You, Lord,*
> *You are our refuge and our fortress;*
> *My God, in You will we trust.* [1]

Abba Father's response displays His great love as He says:

> *Because you have set your love upon Me,*
> *therefore I will deliver you;*

I will set you on high because you have known My name.
You shall call upon Me, and I will answer you;
I will be with you in trouble.
I will honor you in all your ways.[2]
Yes, My children I will show you the path of life;
In My Presence is fullness of joy
At My right hand are pleasures forevermore.[3]

As your journey continues, I challenge you to go beyond the open door the Lord has placed before you. He is inviting you to walk in realms you've never walked in before and exercise His power to fulfill your destiny.

May the Lord bless you and keep you as you continue your journey with Him.

End Notes

Chapter 14

Epilogue

Bibliography

The Journey, Words and Music by LeAnn Squier © 2010, The Darkness Turns CD, Glory of Zion International Ministries, Inc.

Hope of Glory, The Moment CD, spontaneous song © 2011, Glory of Zion International Ministries, Inc.

All Hail the Power of Jesus' Name. Song by Edward Perronet, published 1780 © Public Domain.

Author's Bio

*J*acqueline Varnedoe carries a prophetic mantel and anointing to challenge God's people with the truth and to manifest the grace to do what the Bible says they can do. In her latest book, *OPEN THE DOOR TO MY PRESENCE*, Jacqueline has raised the bar for God's people to make the critical choice whether to hear His voice and enter into a level of intimacy and maturity required to confront today's tumultuous world or to remain in status quo mediocrity. This book ushers readers into the very throne room of Father God as He speaks directly into their hearts in a first-person commentary.

OPEN THE DOOR TO MY PRESENCE completes a trilogy of books including her second book, *JOY CARRIERS*, which ignites the passion in her readers to discover the true joy of the Lord in their daily walk and then inject that joy into the lives of others. This can only be accomplished by walking intimately in His presence day by day. Likewise, Jacqueline's first book, *COME WALK WITH ME*, stirs a greater hunger in God's people for intimacy and passion for the Lord.

In 1995, Jacqueline founded and taught a three-part series of prophetic schools at New Covenant in Thomasville, Georgia and at other churches in the area. In the ensuing years, many people have been motivated and energized in their gifts by attending these schools.

Jacqueline and her husband, Heeth Varnedoe III, founded

the ministry, Calling to Excellence, to help equip, train, and activate the saints in their gifts and callings.

Jacqueline Ponder married Heeth Varnedoe III in 1960 after graduating from the University of Georgia with a Bachelor of Arts degree. Jacqueline was ordained into ministry with Christian International (CI) in 1996 and received her Master's in Biblical Studies with CI in 1999. Jacqueline and Heeth serve on the Board of Governors of CI.

Jacqueline and Heeth are aligned with Glory of Zion International in Corinth, TX and have been commissioned under Apostle Chuck D. Pierce to lead a House of Zion in their home in Thomasville, Georgia.

For information about contacting the author regarding a speaking engagement or to order books including *COME WALK WITH ME*, *JOY CARRIERS*, or *OPEN THE DOOR TO MY PRESENCE*, email Calling to Excellence at varnedoe@rose.net. Amazon carries hardback copies of *COME WALK WITH ME* and *JOY CARRIERS*. *JOY CARRIERS* is available as an EBook on Amazon.com.